D0407482

Funding Provided by
Supervisor Mark DeSaulnier
District IV
Contra Costa County
Board of Supervisors

ULYSSES S.
GRANT

UNION GENERAL AND U.S. PRESIDENT

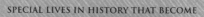

SPECIAL LIVES IN HISTORY THAT BECOME

Signature LIVES

ULYSSES S.

GRANT

UNION GENERAL AND U.S. PRESIDENT

by Brenda Haugen

Content Adviser: John Y. Simon, Ph.D.,
Executive Director and Managing Editor,
Ulysses S. Grant Association

Reading Adviser: Rosemary G. Palmer, Ph.D.,
Department of Literacy, College of Education,
Boise State University

COMPASS POINT BOOKS ✦ MINNEAPOLIS, MINNESOTA

Compass Point Books
3109 West 50th Street, #115
Minneapolis, MN 55410

Visit Compass Point Books on the Internet at *www.compasspointbooks.com*
or e-mail your request to *custserv@compasspointbooks.com*

Editor: Sue Vander Hook
Lead Designer: Jaime Martens
Photo Researcher: Marcie C. Spence
Page Production: Tom Openshaw
Cartographer: XNR Productions, Inc.
Educational Consultant: Diane Smolinski

Managing Editor: Catherine Neitge
Art Director: Keith Griffin
Production Director: Keith McCormick
Creative Director: Terri Foley

To Karen Miller. I'll never take your friendship for granted. *BLH*

Library of Congress Cataloging-in-Publication Data
Haugen, Brenda
    Ulysses S. Grant / by Brenda Haugen.
        p. cm—(Signature lives)
    Includes bibliographical references and index.
    ISBN-13: 978-0-7565-0820-3 (hardcover)
    ISBN-10: 0-7565-0820-7 (hardcover)
    ISBN-13: 978-0-7565-1066-4 (paperback)
    ISBN-10: 0-7565-1066-X (paperback)
    1. Grant, Ulysses S. (Ulysses Simpson), 1822-1885—Juvenile literature.
2. Presidents—United States—Biography—Juvenile literature.
3. Generals—United States—Biography—Juvenile literature. 4. United
States. Army—Biography—Juvenile literature. I. Title. II. Series.
    E672.H376 2004
    973.8'2'092—dc22   2004025342

Signature Lives

CIVIL WAR ERA

The Civil War (1861-1865) split the United States into two countries and divided the people over the issue of slavery. The opposing sides—the Union in the North and the Confederacy in the South—battled each other for four long years in the deadliest American conflict ever fought. The bloody war sometimes pitted family members and friends against each other over the issues of slavery and states' rights. Some of the people who lived and served their country during the Civil War are among the nation's most beloved heroes.

Ulysses S. Grant

Table of Contents

1 FINDING HIS PLACE IN THE WORLD

ന∞ര

Ulysses S. Grant didn't dress up very often, but today was special. He was going to be sworn in as the 18th president of the United States of America.

March 4, 1869, started out cold and rainy in Washington, D.C., but the dreary day couldn't dull the pride and excitement Grant felt. Dressed in his finest black suit, he headed out the door around 9:30 in the morning. He first stopped at Army headquarters where he met his staff. After his new vice president Schuyler Colfax joined him, Grant made his way to the Capitol of the United States.

As Ulysses S. Grant stood in front of the Capitol building, the U.S. Marine Band played joyfully as a huge crowd whooped and cheered. The military fired off a 21-gun salute in honor of the Civil War

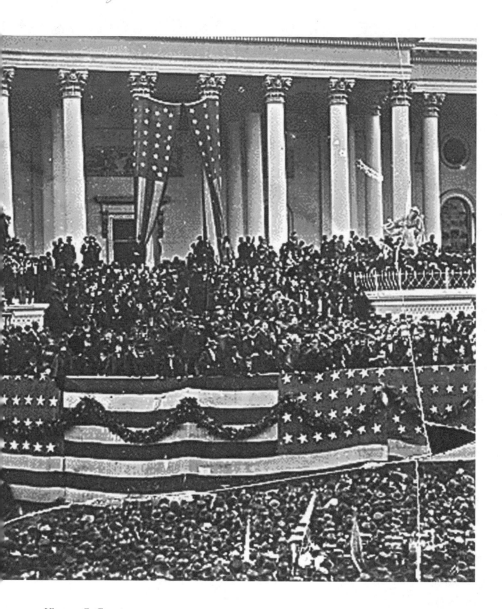

Ulysses S. Grant is sworn in as president of the United States on March 4, 1869, on the steps of the U.S. Capitol.

hero who was about to become president. In fact, Grant's part in the Civil War made this moment in his life possible. Though he never liked the military or war, the battlefield had made Grant famous.

As the new president, Ulysses S. Grant would face many challenges. The states in the South had been severely damaged by the Civil War and needed to be rebuilt. The relationship between the states in the North and the South remained an open wound. Something needed to be done to help the former slaves who now were free.

Even though he had no experience as a politician, Grant was ready to take on the challenges that lay before him. He believed an honest man with his country's best interests at heart could fix the problems it now faced. But while he had proved to be a great leader in battle, would he be as great a leader in the White House? Grant believed the answer to that question was a hearty *yes*, but time would tell.

> *The United States Capitol building is in Washington, D.C. In 1792, William Thornton, a doctor and amateur architect, won a contest to design the building. In 1800, the U.S. Congress started meeting in the Capitol.*

No one who knew Grant in his younger days would have dreamed that he would become president. Even his parents feared that their son, an average student at best, would never amount to much. As a youth, Grant didn't make many close friends. He never really had a passion for anything other than horses.

For much of his life, Grant had no direction. Unlike his brothers, Grant rejected the idea of

The Ulysses S. Grant Memorial in Washington, D.C.

going into the tannery business with his father. Yet he couldn't seem to find anything he liked or was particularly good at doing. He tried and failed at farming. He tried and failed at managing his own business.

Ulysses S. Grant's life changed, however, when

he went to war for his country. He discovered he had great military skills, and he was deeply committed to the principles of the United States. He was a patriot and would do whatever he could to defend the unity of his country.

His passion and loyalty were greatly tested during the bloodiest war ever fought by the United States—the Civil War. Grant served in the U.S. Army, eventually becoming the country's top general in charge of leading the war against the South. Union General Ulysses S. Grant was the man to whom Confederate General Robert E. Lee would surrender, helping to end the war that tore the young country in two. Grant, the popular military hero, would go on to serve his country as president for eight years. ☙

2 GROWING UP

❧✦❧

Jesse Root Grant and his wife, Hannah Simpson Grant, welcomed their first child into the world on April 27, 1822, at their home in Point Pleasant, Ohio. Yet they couldn't agree on a name. They decided to enlist the help of relatives, who put their suggestions on pieces of paper and dropped them into a hat.

Jesse Grant pulled a small piece of paper out of the hat and saw the name Ulysses. He shook his head, not liking the name at all. Again he put his hand into the hat and drew out another name—Hiram. This one, he believed, fit his newborn son.

Hannah Grant and her mother thought Ulysses should be the child's name, since it was the first one drawn out of the hat. Jesse agreed that Ulysses could be the child's middle name, but he preferred

The Grant tannery business was located in these buildings across the street from the family's home.

Hiram as a first name and put his foot down regarding the issue. Hiram's mother and grandmother consented, but insisted on calling the boy by his middle name. Soon everyone knew him just as Ulysses, Lyss for short, and many assumed it was his first name.

When Ulysses was a year and a half old, his family moved to a nice brick house in Georgetown, Ohio. This place remained his home until 1839, when he was 17 years old. His two brothers and three sisters were born here. Ulysses was just 3 years old when his brother Samuel Simpson came into the world. By the time the youngest of the children, Mary Frances, was born, Ulysses was 17. While their mother stayed home and took care of the family and their home, their father Jesse went to work right across the street.

Ulysses S. Grant grew up around his father's business. Jesse owned a tannery, where animal hides were made into leather. He hoped Ulysses would follow in his footsteps, but Ulysses didn't like killing animals to get the hides, and he hated the sight of blood. It didn't help that the business stunk so badly that the Grants could smell it in their home across the street. No, the tannery business wasn't for him, Ulysses decided.

Jesse Grant also owned and farmed a lot of land. Ulysses liked farming, especially the work done with horses. At a young age, he was driving a horse-drawn wagon to help out on the farm. Ulysses later wrote:

> *When I was seven or eight years of age, I began hauling wood used in the house and shops, I could not load it on the wag-*

Ulysses S. Grant's mother was a strong, religious woman who kept quiet most of the time. She would read only one newspaper—the Christian Advocate—*a religious publication from Cincinnati. Some people think Grant inherited his strength of character from his mother.*

ons, of course, at that time, but I could drive, and the choppers would load, and some one at the house unload.

By age 11, Ulysses was strong enough to guide a horse-drawn plow as it broke up the soil. He also gladly cared for several horses and a cow or two after attending school every day. Willing to do anything to avoid working in the tannery, Ulysses used his skill with horses to earn money working for Georgetown families who needed carriage drivers.

Not only did Ulysses love horses, they responded well to him. He enjoyed having horses of his own. One particular horse caught his eye, and Ulysses decided he must have the beautiful creature. The colt was owned by a man named Mr. Ralston. Grant later told about the memorable incident.

My father had offered twenty dollars for it, but Ralston wanted twenty-five. I was so anxious to have the colt, that after the owner left, I begged to be allowed to take him at the price demanded. My father yielded, but said twenty dollars was all the horse was worth, and told me to offer that price; if it was not accepted I was to offer twenty-two and a half, and if that would not get him, to give the twenty-five. I at once mounted a horse and went for the colt. When I got to Mr. Ralston's house, I said to him: 'Papa says I may offer you twenty dollars for the colt, but if you won't take that, I am to offer twenty-two and a half, and if you won't take that, I am to give you twenty-five.' It would not require a Connecticut man to guess the price finally agreed upon.

The story illustrated his love for animals, but it also showed he wasn't very good at business. Both of these facts would be true for his entire life. The

Ulysses S. Grant owned many horses, but his favorite was Cincinnati.

incident caused Ulysses a great deal of embarrassment. Throughout his life, he found people willing to take advantage of his honest nature. However, he never quit trusting people.

Ulysses S. Grant attended school mostly in Georgetown, Ohio. A small, skinny boy, Ulysses often found himself in trouble with his teachers. Yet when that happened, he took responsibility for his poor behavior and didn't complain about any punishments his instructors handed out.

Ulysses S. Grant spent most of his early years in Georgetown, Ohio, and later built a home for his family in St. Louis, Missouri.

Grant's parents thought Ulysses might be more successful in a different school. When he turned 14, Ulysses went to Maysville, Kentucky, where he lived with relatives and attended the Richeson and Rand School. The next year, Ulysses once again changed schools, this time attending a private school in Ripley, Ohio. Although not very studious, he loved to read and showed skill in his math classes.

Jesse Grant still worried about his firstborn son. His two younger sons, Simpson and Orvil, already were showing interest in his tanning business. His daughters Clara, Jennie, and Mary would live at home until they married. As Ulysses got older, however, he still had no idea what career suited him. What would he do when he finished school?

When Jesse heard there was a vacancy at the U.S. Military Academy at West Point, New York, he decided that's where Ulysses should go. Ulysses didn't want to go, but his father ignored his protests. Not only would the academy provide a free education, his father said, it would also set the path for his future. The connections Ulysses would make at such a fine school and the important things he would learn would no doubt ensure his success as an adult. If Ulysses didn't discover another occupation at the academy, he surely would have a lifelong career in the military.

Not just anyone can go to West Point. Officials

Cadets at the U.S. Military Academy at West Point, New York, in the 1850s

such as a member of the U.S. Congress must nominate a student for admission. Congressman Thomas Hamer of Ohio had the right to appoint students to West Point. But Hamer and Jesse Grant didn't agree politically. So Jesse wrote a letter to Senator Thomas Morris of Ohio, asking that his son Ulysses be considered for nomination to the academy. Morris probably turned Jesse's letter over to Hamer, because Ulysses soon received an appointment from the congressman.

Hamer quickly filled out the proper forms for the appointment. He was in such a hurry that he made a mistake on Ulysses's name. Instead of writing Hiram Ulysses Grant, he wrote Ulysses S. Grant. Hamer likely knew the young man as Ulysses, not Hiram. When he needed to account for a middle name, he put *S* for Simpson, which was Ulysses's mother's last name before she married Jesse Grant.

When he got to the academy and realized the mistake, Ulysses decided to become Ulysses S. Grant rather than fill out a lot of papers to correct the error. Besides, he wasn't very fond of his name. He welcomed the error because the other students might tease him about his real initials—H.U.G. Now he was U.S. Grant, and that fit him better.

When some students at West Point saw the name U.S. Grant on the school roster, they guessed at what the initials represented. One student thought they stood for Uncle Sam, a nickname for the government of the United States. From then on, Grant's nickname at West Point was Sam. ❧

3 WEST POINT

ം⧽⧼ം

When school started at West Point in 1839, Ulysses S. Grant looked more like a boy than a young man. With sandy brown hair and freckles, the 17-year-old stood just 5-feet-1-inch tall and weighed only 117 pounds.

Shy and quiet, Grant made few close friends at his new school. Content to fall in the middle of the pack as far as his grades were concerned, he didn't fit in with the young men who worked hard to achieve high scores. He didn't fit in with those who wanted military careers once they graduated, either.

"A military life had no charms for me," Grant wrote. In fact, Grant found West Point boring. He didn't like his French class, which showed in his very poor grade in that subject. He spent most of his time reading novels. Since he excelled in math, Grant

West Point Academy, shown in the 1860s, is located about 50 miles (80.5 km) north of New York City along the Hudson River.

thought perhaps he could be a math teacher someday. First, though, he would have to graduate. "I had not the faintest desire to stay in the army even if I should be graduated, which I did not expect," Grant wrote.

Daily life at West Point proved difficult for Ulysses S. Grant. Eventually, though, life at the military academy improved for him. He got used to all the rules and took some classes in horsemanship, which he liked very much. His skill with horses surpassed the skills of some of his teachers. Grant started thinking that maybe he could join the cavalry if a career as a math teacher didn't work out.

Artillery practice at West Point in the 1850s

During his third year at West Point, Grant earned the rank of sergeant. As an officer, he was expected to command the privates below him, but Grant despised military life and disliked ordering people around. The new rank wouldn't last long. Since he received too many marks against him for misconduct that year, Grant was reduced to the rank of private for his fourth year.

> *The United States Military Academy at West Point, New York, has educated some of the country's top leaders. Among them are Robert E. Lee, whom Ulysses S. Grant fought against in the Civil War, and Dwight D. Eisenhower, who served as President from 1953–1961.*

Yet he did make it to his senior year. As his graduation from West Point drew near, however, Grant became ill with a very bad cough. He thought he had contracted tuberculosis, a disease that had killed others in his family.

Soon Grant was a sickly 117 pounds again, the same weight he had been when he started school four years earlier. Since he had grown 6 inches taller in that time, he looked terribly thin. Grant's illness turned out to be a bad cough called Tyler's grippe—not tuberculosis—and he soon recovered. He graduated from West Point in 1843 at the age of 21. Academically, he ranked 21st in his graduating class of 39 students.

4 JULIA AND THE WAR WITH MEXICO

Chapter

❧

After graduating from West Point, Ulysses S. Grant started his military service as a second lieutenant with the 4th U.S. Infantry. He would have rather been a math teacher or a member of the cavalry, but now he was in the Army—exactly what he had hoped to avoid.

Grant's regiment was stationed near St. Louis, Missouri. He found that he didn't really fit in with most of the men there, but Grant did have one friendly place he could go. Frederick Dent had been Grant's roommate their last year at the academy, and they had gotten along well. Dent's family happened to live in the St. Louis area, and Grant spent much of his free time there.

The Dents lived a life unfamiliar to Grant—they

U.S. soldiers entered Mexico City on September 14, 1847, during the Mexican War.

were slave owners who ran a large plantation called White Haven in the St. Louis area. Grant's father was strictly against slavery.

Grant particularly liked Frederick's 17-year-old sister, Julia. She recently had graduated from a private school and was living at White Haven. A strong girl with striking blue eyes, Julia loved horseback riding as much as Grant did. While she took pains to prove she was a proper lady, Julia also enjoyed outdoor activities like fishing with her brothers. At that time, refined ladies didn't do these kinds of activities. Julia wrote about one fishing experience:

> *Oh! What happiness to see that nibble, to feel the pull, and to see the plunge of the cork; then the little quivering, shining creature was landed high on the bank.*

Ulysses and Julia fell in love right away. They spent as much time together as they could and enjoyed dancing and going on walks together. Soon, Grant found out his regiment was heading to Louisiana. He was to join his fellow soldiers at once. But before he did, Grant decided to stop at White Haven to see Julia. He planned to propose.

When Grant reached White Haven, he was drenched. A creek he had to cross was deeper than usual from the rainy weather. He couldn't avoid getting soaking wet as he crossed the creek. Not want-

A barn at White Haven, the Dent family plantation in St. Louis, Missouri

ing to look messy when proposing to Julia, Grant borrowed a suit that belonged to his friend Frederick. In a suit that was dry but didn't really fit, Grant proposed to 19-year-old Julia. Her answer was a happy *yes*.

The couple agreed to keep their engagement a secret until Grant could return and ask for her father's permission. For now, Grant was off to join his regiment in Louisiana, which was heading out to fight with Mexico in a battle over Texas.

In the 1820s, Americans pushed west and began settling in the Texas area. In 1836, settlers declared their independence from Mexico. Four years later, the American government annexed Texas, making it part of the United States. But Mexico wouldn't give

Lieutenant Ulysses S. Grant (left) and General Alexander Hays during the Mexican War.

up the land without a fight.

While Grant believed the United States should not take Texas away from Mexico, his duty to his country came first. He was called upon to fight against Mexico, and that is exactly what he did.

In September 1845, Grant and the rest of the 4th Infantry set sail from New Orleans, Louisiana, and traveled to Corpus Christi, Texas. Though he was not happy about fighting in a war, Grant was eager to follow General Zachary Taylor, the admired commander of the American troops and someone Grant liked. Taylor stayed calm, no matter what the situation, and he didn't complain. He also stated his mission clearly. Grant appreciated Taylor's plain talk.

Zachary Taylor (1784-1850) served in the Army for 40 years. A quiet and friendly leader, Taylor never lost a battle. His troops nicknamed him "Old Rough and Ready." In 1849, when slavery was dividing the country, Taylor became the 12th president of the United States. Taylor wanted to deal with the slavery issue but became ill and died. He was president for just 16 months.

> *Taylor was not a conversationalist, but on paper he could put his meaning so plainly that there could be no mistaking it.*

Taylor acted like one of the guys, not a stuffy leader who thought he was better than everyone

Map shows the U.S. territory acquired from Mexico as a result of the Mexican War.

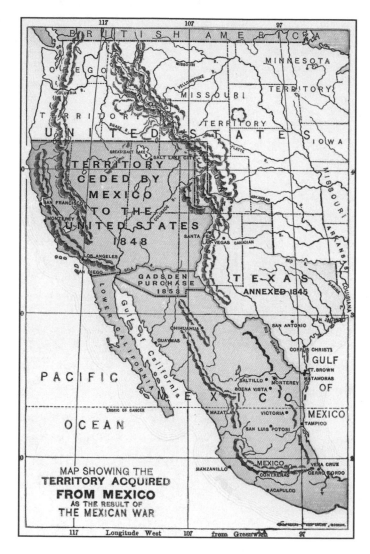

MAP SHOWING THE
TERRITORY ACQUIRED
FROM MEXICO
AS THE RESULT OF
THE MEXICAN WAR

else. Grant tried to be one of the guys, too. Even though he never liked killing animals, Grant agreed to join a friend on a turkey hunt. Grant later told about the day of the hunt.

*We had scarcely reached the edge of the
timber when I heard the flutter of wings
overhead, and in an instant I saw two or
three turkeys flying away. These were
soon followed by more, then more, and
more, until a flock of twenty or thirty
had left just over my head. All this time
I stood watching the turkeys to see where
they flew—with my gun on my shoulder,
and never once thought of leveling it at
the birds.*

Grant enjoyed the outdoors, even when he was at
war. The land the 4th Infantry saw during the
Mexican War was filled with wildlife. Grant delighted
in seeing huge herds of wild horses. Deer, antelope,
turkeys, and other wild creatures were common
sights, as well. While many of his fellow soldiers
enjoyed the good hunting the animals provided,
Grant took in the beautiful view. He shared his
thoughts in a letter to Julia:

*I wish you could be here to take one of
these rides with me and see the beautiful
Valley of Mexico. The whole Valley is
spread out to the view covered with
numerous lakes, green fields, and little
Villages and to all appearances it would
be a short ride to go around the whole valley in a day, but you would find that it
would take a week.*

Grant served as his infantry's quartermaster—a huge responsibility. His job was to load and direct wagon trains and pack mules that carried supplies to the soldiers. He made sure that food, clothing, and equipment reached his regiment. If he didn't do his job, the troops didn't stand a chance of winning any battles. The 4th Infantry crossed rough mountainous territory during the war, which made a hard job even more difficult.

Grant soon wanted a promotion to a position higher than quartermaster, so he asked to go to the front lines to fight. While his request was turned down, he did participate in the fighting before the end of the Mexican War. During the final battle in Mexico City, Grant demonstrated his clever military skill. Seeing a church tower that overlooked the whole city, he knew it would make a great place to launch an attack.

Arriving at the tower, Grant found the stairs were too narrow to allow a cannon to pass. He told the soldiers to remove the cannon from the carriage, take it apart, and carry it up the stairs in pieces. At the top, they reassembled it and readied for battle. Grant's plan worked and shocked the enemy. His quick thinking earned him the praise of his superiors.

In the autumn of 1847, when Grant was 25 years old, fighting in the Mexican War ended. The peace treaty, signed February 2, 1848, gave the United

Ulysses S. Grant and his soldiers launch an attack from a church tower in Mexico City.

States the land that is now Texas, Utah, Nevada, and California, as well as parts of New Mexico, Arizona, Colorado, and Wyoming. In exchange, the United States agreed to pay Mexico $15 million for the land and $3 million in damage claims American citizens made against the Mexican government.

Ulysses S. Grant was pleased with the victory,

Ulysses S. Grant and his wife Julia Dent Grant, circa 1860

but he looked forward to going back to Julia. He wanted to ask her father's permission for them to marry. Unfortunately, the Grant and Dent families were not very excited about the couple's plan to get married.

Julia Dent's father didn't think Ulysses S. Grant had much of a future, and he thought Grant lacked ambition. However, Julia had her heart set on Ulysses, and her father agreed to the match, in spite of his disappointment.

Jesse Grant wasn't happy about his son's engagement, either. Dent was a slaveholder, and Jesse hated slavery. He surely did not want to be related, even through marriage, to a family that defended slavery. However, Jesse would learn to put up with their ideas and opinions.

Ulysses S. Grant and Julia Dent were married August 22, 1848, in St. Louis, Missouri. After the marriage, Grant stayed in the Army. But now, Julia traveled with him most of the time. ॐ

5 STRUGGLING BETWEEN WARS

❧✦❧

A few months after Ulysses and Julia Grant were married, the Army assigned Grant to Sackets Harbor, New York. The Grants lived along the shores of Lake Ontario, where it was scenic but cold. A few months later, the Army transferred Grant to Detroit, Michigan. On May 30, 1850, Julia Grant gave birth to the couple's first child, a son named Frederick.

The following year, Ulysses and Julia were not disappointed when Grant was shuffled back to Sackets Harbor. They realized how much they had missed that beautiful town.

By the spring of 1852, Grant received his orders that he was being transferred to Fort Vancouver, Washington, a trading post on the Pacific Coast. No direct land route existed between the developed

Today, the Atlantic
and Pacific oceans are
connected by the
Panama Canal. The
United States built the
waterway, finishing it
in 1914. The canal cut
thousands of miles off
trips made by ships
traveling from one
coast of the United
States to the other.

East and the West Coast. Grant didn't want to put his family in danger by taking them on a long, rugged journey across this vast frontier. His son Frederick was only 2 years old, and Julia was pregnant with their second child. Rather than risk their health, Grant sent them to St. Louis to stay with the Dents.

Grant then boarded a ship in New York bound for the Pacific Coast. On the first leg of his trip, he enjoyed the sights of the ocean, even seeing a group of whales along the way. However, crossing the Isthmus of Panama, a small strip of mosquito-infested jungle that separated the Atlantic and Pacific oceans, was more dangerous.

The Panama jungle was humid and hot. Grant arrived during the rainy season, a miserable and muddy time of year. Many soldiers became ill with cholera, but Grant put his leadership skills to work. He set up two hospitals, one in a ship beached on the shore and another inside tents on a nearby island.

Meanwhile, back home with her family in St. Louis, Julia was ready to give birth to their second child. To Grant's disappointment, he couldn't be in St. Louis on July 22, 1852, to welcome his baby son

Ulysses S. Grant Jr. into the world.

Having done all he could in Panama, Grant continued his trip to Fort Vancouver. Once there, he made some friends, but that was not enough to keep him from growing very lonely. He longed to see his wife and children, especially the infant son he had never met.

Grant used his free time to work on ways to make extra money, which he planned to use to reunite with his family. None of his work paid off, though. He planted potatoes, but a flood ruined the

Ulysses S. Grant was very lonely during his military service at Fort Vancouver, Washington.

The four Grant children: Frederick, Ulysses Jr., Ellen, and Jesse

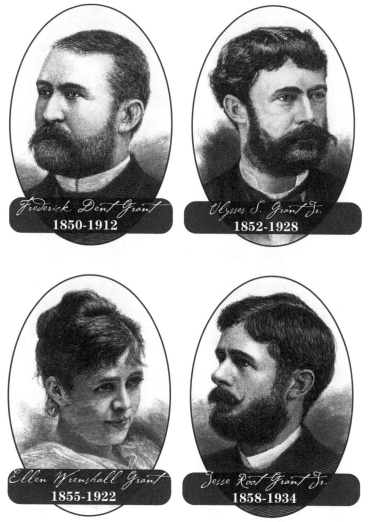

Frederick Dent Grant
1850–1912

Ulysses S. Grant Jr.
1852–1928

Ellen Wrenshall Grant
1855–1922

Jesse Root Grant Jr.
1858–1934

crop. He went into business with a merchant he knew, but the money Grant invested disappeared along with the merchant. As the disappointments piled up, Grant grew dejected and discouraged.

Although Ulysses S. Grant was promoted to captain in 1853, the new position wasn't enough to cheer him up. Early in 1854, he was transferred to Fort Humboldt on the coast of northern California, which turned out to be an even more lonely place for Grant. At least at Fort Vancouver he had friends. At Fort Humboldt, he felt as if he had no friends at all.

Oregon became a state February 14, 1859. The area remained a rather wild frontier, though. Overland travel to Oregon proved difficult and time consuming, and a railroad connection was still more than 20 years away.

"I do nothing but set in my room and read and occasionally take a short ride on one of the public horses," Grant wrote in a letter to Julia. He had grown tired of being away from his family. His second son was now nearly 2 years old, and he hadn't seen him yet. When Grant's new superior officer proved to be a mean-tempered man, Grant decided he had had enough. He asked for a transfer. When his request was denied, Grant resigned from the Army and packed to go home to Julia and his children. Grant later explained in his memoirs:

> *My family all this while, was at the East. It consisted now of a wife and two children. I saw no chance of supporting them on the Pacific coast out of my pay as an army officer, I concluded therefore to resign.*

Grant's resignation angered his father, who again worried about how his son would support himself and his family. Jesse Grant believed his son was making a big mistake and tried to convince him to change his mind. Grant's mind was made up. He was coming home.

Now, at the age of 32, Grant faced a new challenge. He had to find work and earn money to support his family. In the spring of 1855, Grant planted a crop on his brother-in-law Lewis Dent's farm. Julia raised chickens—some to butcher and some for their eggs—which she enjoyed.

Soon, Julia's father let the couple use some of his land in St. Louis to build a house. Grant worked hard to clear a space and cut enough timber to build a home for his family on the plot. He also created a clearing for a field where he could grow crops.

Ulysses S. Grant proudly finished his home in 1856. Almost every farm in the area had a name, usually an important sounding one. Grant chose the name Hardscrabble for his home, which means a bare living achieved by hard labor. While Grant was pleased with the house he'd built with his own hands, Julia hated it. To her, it was nothing more than a cabin. She wanted the finer things of life. For now, though, Hardscrabble was the best Grant could do.

On the land, Grant planted crops of oats, potatoes, and corn. But despite all his farming efforts, he didn't make a profit on the crops. To earn more

Hardscrabble, the home built by Ulysses S. Grant in St. Louis, Missouri

money during the winter months, Grant turned to selling firewood on the street corners of St. Louis.

Times were tough for the Grant family and wouldn't get easier anytime soon. Although Grant had built the family's home, it sat on land owned by Julia's father. Grant worked hard to support his wife and children, but the family often relied on Dent for money when they couldn't pay their bills. Grant even asked his own father for help in a letter he wrote to him in February 1857:

Spring is approaching when farmers require not only to till the soil, but to have the wherewith to till it, and to seed it. To this end I am going to make the last appeal to you. I do this because . . . you voluntarily offered to give me a Thousand dollars, to commence with, and because there is no one els[e] to whom I could, with the same propriety, apply. It is always usual for parents to give their children assistince in begining life (and I am only begining, though thirty five years of age, nearly) and what I ask is not much.

After another season of failure, Grant and his family moved into the Dent plantation at White Haven. Julia's mother had died, and Dent decided to move into the heart of St. Louis rather than live 12 miles (19.3 km) from town. He turned the operation over to his son-in-law. Grant did his best to run the plantation, but he again found himself failing at farming and wondering what to do with his life.

Soon, Grant moved his family into the city of St. Louis, where he worked with Julia's cousin Harry Boggs as a rent collector. He hated the job more than anything he had ever done. Feeling like a failure, Grant packed up his family in 1860 and moved them to Galena, Illinois. There, his father Jesse Grant had opened up a leather goods store. Grant's brothers, Simpson and Orvil, ran the business and agreed that their older brother could work there as

Ulysses S. Grant and his family, circa 1867

a clerk. Earning only $50 a month, Grant still did his job well and appreciated the steady paycheck. But it surprised no one that he wasn't happy with the clerk position.

Grant wouldn't be truly happy until he found himself immersed again in the responsibilities of war—the Civil War. ℘

6 THE COUNTRY DIVIDES

Chapter

ᕱᕲᕱ

For years, the United States had been growing apart. Northern and Southern states were very different from each other. Also, some states believed the federal government was growing too powerful and taking away rights from the states.

The Northern states consisted mainly of small farms and industries. European immigrants flooding into Boston, New York, and Philadelphia were a great source of cheap labor. In the Southern states, agriculture prospered. With a longer growing season than their northern neighbors, Southerners planted a wide variety of crops. Cotton and tobacco took longer to grow, and the South, with its warm weather, was a good place to plant them. The small farmer as well as the large plantation owner benefited from good crops.

Farmers bring large bales of cotton to the marketplace in a Georgia town in the mid-1800s.

But planting, caring for, and picking cotton and tobacco meant a great deal of backbreaking work. Immigrants weren't coming to the South in droves as they were in the North. The Northern cities were bigger, and there were many job opportunities in factories. Farmers and plantation owners in the North and the South needed a lot of workers to keep their operations going. So they turned to slave labor.

For several centuries, millions of Africans had been captured and shipped to North and South America. In the United States, about 4 million black

A white overseer watches black slaves in the cotton fields to make sure they are working hard.

slaves were working in the South by 1860. Many people believed slavery was wrong, but most Southerners also believed it was a necessary evil.

Many people in the South saw that slavery was very profitable. In time, they even considered it a good thing. A group of people in the North called abolitionists began a movement to try to end slavery. Slavery became the center of intense conflicts between the North and the South. Soon, states in the South were considering breaking away from the United States and forming a country of their own.

On December 10, 1860, Grant wrote to a friend in St. Louis about the problem:

> *It is hard to realize that a State or States should commit so suicidal an act as to secede from the Union yet from all the reports I have no doubt but that at least five of them will do it.*

The issue became heated during the presidential campaign of 1860. Many Southerners considered Republican presidential candidate Abraham Lincoln a threat to their way of life. They believed the man from Illinois would end slavery if he were elected to office. Southerners warned they would secede from the Union if Lincoln became president.

Lincoln won the election, and the Southern states followed through with their threats. South

Abraham Lincoln was inaugurated as president of the United States on March 4, 1861.

Carolina seceded from the United States in December 1860. Alabama, Florida, Louisiana, Georgia, and Mississippi left the Union a month later. In time, five more states joined what they called the Confederate States of America.

Lincoln tried to avoid war but said the Union would not be broken. He said he would use force to hold on to federally owned military posts in the South. But on April 12, 1861, Confederate forces fired on a U.S. fort—Fort Sumter in Charleston, South Carolina. The Union fought back—the Civil War had begun.

On April 16, just four days later, the news about the battle at Fort Sumter reached Galena, Illinois. A town meeting was called, and Grant—the only one present who had professional Army training—led the proceedings. Grant said he felt a duty to help preserve the Union, and he immediately started enlisting local men to help in the war effort.

After 11 Southern states seceded from the Union, they set up their own country called the Confederate States of America. Richmond, Virginia, was named the capital, and a constitution was approved in March 1861. Jefferson Davis became the first president of the Confederate states.

While he felt clear in his duty, Grant found himself at odds with his father-in-law. Dent did not believe federal power should be used to stop Southern states from seceding. Grant didn't hesitate to tell him the Union must be saved. If the South insisted on breaking away, the North's greater population would crush the rebellion and slavery with it, he warned. On April 19, Grant wrote:

> *The times are indee[d] startling but now is the time, particularly in the border*

Slave states, for men to prove their love of country. In all this I can but see the doom of Slavery.

While a war raged, Grant predicted, other countries would step in and produce cotton while the South was busy fighting. After the war, he said, the South would have tough competition in the cotton

Ulysses S. Grant owned several large, strong horses that he rode into battle during the Civil War.

market, which it didn't have now.

As Grant worked to recruit volunteers, he believed that any day he would get a message from the U.S. War Department. He expected his service in the Mexican War would certainly guarantee him a higher position in the Union Army than just working with volunteers. But that message never came.

It took the efforts of Illinois Congressman Elihu Washburne to get Grant appointed to the rank of colonel. Right away, Grant was given the challenge of leading the 21st Illinois Regiment, a group of rowdy volunteers. Grant approached the challenge with gusto. Putting his experiences at West Point and in the Mexican War to good use, Grant insisted on order.

Soon, his volunteer troops were in shape and ready for battle. Grant would later remember:

> *My men behaved admirably, and the lesson has been a good one for them. They can now go into camp after a day's march with as much promptness as veteran troops; they can strike their tents and be on the march with equal celerity.*

His hard work did not go unrewarded. President Lincoln presented a list of 26 names to Congress on July 31, 1861. He wanted these men promoted to brigadier general. Grant's name was on the list.

Grant fired off a letter of thanks to Washburne. He knew Washburne had likely brought his name to the attention of the president. Grant appreciated the confidence Washburne and the people of Illinois had in him. Grant wrote to Julia in Galena:

> *I certainly feel very greatful to the people of Illinois for the interest they seem to have taken in me and unasked to. Whilst I was about Springfield I certainly never blew my own trumpet and was not aware that I attracted any attention but it seems from what I have heard from there the people, who were perfect strangers to me up the commencement of our present unhappy national difficulties, were very unanimous in recommending me for my present position. I shall do my very best not to disappoint them.*

Of all the people in Grant's life, Julia remained the one who always had confidence in him. She was proud of him no matter what happened, but it was difficult to see him go off to war again. Remembering her lonely days during the Mexican War and the time Grant was on the Pacific Coast, Julia wished she could go with her husband on his travels.

While that was out of the question, she did send their 11-year-old son Frederick. Grant enjoyed having Frederick around, but when the regiment was done drilling and likely to see some action, he quickly sent the boy back home to Galena. "He did not want to go at all," Grant wrote to Julia, "and I felt loathe at sending him but now we are in the enemies country I thought you would be alarmed if he was with me."

Grant marched with his men to Cairo, Illinois, where he set up headquarters. Cairo's location where the Mississippi and Ohio rivers meet made it an important military location. Just a few miles away, the Tennessee and Cumberland rivers joined the Ohio. Grant's mission was to stop the Confederates from moving north on any of these waterways.

The young leader was not content idly protecting these rivers, though. Wanting to march south, Grant decided his troops would take Paducah, Kentucky,

Union soldiers camped outside the city of Cairo, Illinois, readying for battle.

a town at the mouth of the Tennessee River. He accomplished this task without a fight.

His next plan was to take Belmont, Missouri. There, on November 7, 1861, Grant suffered his first defeat. After a bloody battle, he felt guilty for being the one responsible for ordering so many men to their deaths.

Still, Grant chose to press onward, hoping to invade the South by striking Fort Henry along the Tennessee River. When Grant presented his idea to Henry Wager Halleck, his superior officer, Halleck said no. Halleck didn't like or trust Grant. In fact, Halleck saw him as a possible threat to his command.

Union soldiers fought the Battle of Fort Henry from their boats positioned on the Tennessee River.

On the other hand, Halleck did respect Andrew Hull Foote, a naval officer who believed in Grant and his plan. In support of Grant's idea, Foote wrote

to Halleck:

> *Grant and myself are of opinion that Fort*
> *Henry on the Tennessee can be carried*
> *with four Iron-clad Gun-boats and troops*
> *to be permanent occupied. Have we your*
> *authority to move for that purpose?*

Halleck gave the mission his blessing—as long as Foote was part of it. On February 3, 1862, Foote went upstream with seven gunboats toward Fort Henry. Grant sent about 16,000 soldiers on ships that followed Foote's lead. Three days later, the battle began. Union gunboats fired on Fort Henry for two hours, causing a great deal of damage. Perhaps the most important hit was on the fort's cannon.

As Grant's troops fought their way forward, Confederate General Lloyd Tilghman couldn't maintain control of the fort and surrendered, along with 70 of his injured men. But he had already sent 2,500 soldiers to help hold Fort Donelson just 11 miles (17.7 km) away. Fort Donelson stood as the next logical target of attack, and Tilghman knew it.

Grant wanted to head to Fort Donelson right away. He sent a telegram to Halleck letting him know of the fall of Fort Henry and his desire to take Fort Donelson. Even President Lincoln was urging Halleck to move his troops on to Fort Donelson.

"Our success or failure at Donelson is vastly

important," Lincoln wrote to Halleck, "and I beg you to put your soul into the effort."

Grant quickly learned Halleck would be slow in moving on requests for action, and the two would disagree many times during the war because of it. In the case of Fort Donelson, Grant took control and moved ahead on his own.

On February 14, 1862, Union gunboats took aim at Fort Donelson. The Confederates fought back fiercely. As the fort burned, the rebels continued firing at the gunboats until the boats were so badly damaged, they became useless. The rebels also held off Union troops attacking the back of the fort.

The capture of Fort Donelson, Tennessee, by Ulysses S. Grant's Union forces in 1862

Enraged, Grant forced his troops to regroup. They would not be defeated. Union soldiers battled

the enemy back into the fort and began a siege, surrounding the fort and blocking any chance the Confederates had to get supplies. If soldiers trapped in Fort Donelson wouldn't surrender, they would starve. Eventually, the Confederates chose to surrender, and Grant's troops captured 15,000 men and an important section of the Cumberland River. Grant wrote in one of his letters to Julia, "This is the largest capture I believe ever made on the continent."

With momentum on their side, Grant believed Union forces should keep pushing into enemy territory. "I am growing anxious to know what the next move is going to be," he wrote to Halleck.

Yet Halleck didn't want Grant to accomplish any more great victories and make a better reputation for himself. President Lincoln was taking notice of the ambitious soldier. He paid attention to the difficult Union victories and didn't want to stop the progress troops were making.

For his efforts at Fort Donelson, Lincoln pro-

Ulysses S. Grant's nickname was "Unconditional Surrender Grant"—a name his troops gave him after the battle at Fort Donelson. The Confederate forces, blockaded inside the fort, asked for terms of surrender. Grant refused to negotiate. He would accept only unconditional and total surrender. The Confederates were left with no other choice than to accept Grant's terms. The Confederates surrendered there—unconditionally.

Major Allan Pinkerton (left) meets with President Lincoln and General John A. McClernand at a Civil War encampment.

moted Grant to major general. Halleck also asked for a promotion but was ignored. Growing more jealous of Grant and less willing to listen to his plans, Halleck tried to get Grant in trouble. Halleck sent a letter to George B. McClellan, commanding general in Washington, D.C.:

> *I have no communication with General Grant for more than a week. He left his command without my authority and went to Nashville. It is hard to censure a successful general immediately after a victory,*

*but I think he richly deserves it. I can
get no returns, no reports, no information of any kind from him. Satisfied
with victory, he sits down and enjoys it
without any regard to the future. I am
worn out and tired with this neglect
and inefficiency.*

McClellan did not hesitate to reply:

*The future success of our cause demands
that proceedings such as Grant's should at
once be checked. Generals must observe
discipline as well as private soldiers. Do
not hesitate to arrest him at once if the
good of the service requires it, and place
C. F. Smith in command.*

Halleck could not have been more pleased with
the general's response. Quickly, he informed Grant
in a telegram to stay at Fort Henry and place Major
General C. F. Smith in command of the expedition.
Grant grew angry as he read the message and sent
back a telegram saying he had followed orders. The
only reason he had not given Halleck information
regarding troop numbers was because Charles
Smith had yet to report his numbers to Grant. This
was the same Charles Smith who was to take over
Grant's command.

Despite his anger, Grant did as he was told. On
March 5, 1862, he reluctantly turned over his com-

mand of the Tennessee River expedition to Smith. Halleck sent another telegram, which Grant received on March 6.

> *Your neglect of repeated orders to report the strength of your command has created great dissatisfaction, & seriously interfered with military plans. Your going to Nashville without authority & when your presence with your troops was of the utmost importance, was a matter of very serious complaint at Washington, so much so that I was advised to arrest you on your return.*

Grant had enough. In a return telegram, he denied these claims and sent a copy to Congressman Washburne. The Illinois Republican brought the matter to the attention of another important Illinois Republican—President Abraham Lincoln.

The president agreed with Grant—the Union needed to press on and defeat the Confederate rebels. Lincoln, too, was tired of Halleck's slow approach. Lincoln told Halleck to either present evidence of Grant's ineffectiveness or to leave him alone. While Halleck continued to hold Grant back, he stopped making charges that Grant wasn't doing his duty.

Grant wanted the war to be over. In the early days of the war, he believed what many believed—the conflict would end quickly, and the Union would be

restored. As the days slowly turned into years, these optimists were proved wrong.

Grant came to realize the South would only be defeated through continued force. The rebels weren't going to give up until they were beaten so badly that they had no choice. Because the North had a larger population, it had more soldiers. Its strength was truly in its numbers. Grant predicted a bloody war ahead with a body count that would continue to rise. His belief about the future sadly became the country's reality. 🞉

Union and Confederate forces would continue to fight, including the fierce Battle of Corinth in Mississippi, on October 4, 1862, resulting in a Union victory.

7 SHILOH, VICKSBURG, AND RICHMOND

Chapter

❧✦❧

Ulysses S. Grant would not be held back any longer. He returned to his troops in March 1862 and took back his command at Pittsburg Landing on the Tennessee River. It was here, however, that Grant would be surprised in battle.

About three weeks later, Confederates attacked the Union camp at Shiloh near Pittsburg Landing. As Grant was eating breakfast just 9 miles (14.5 km) away, he heard the first shots fired. Shocked, Grant quickly jumped in a boat and headed to Pittsburg Landing. Along the way he shouted to one of his officers, Lew Wallace, to march his men immediately to Shiloh.

At the battle that raged at Shiloh, Grant faced one of the finest officers of the Confederate Army—

General Ulysses S. Grant at a Union camp

General Albert Sidney Johnston. The first day of fighting was a bloodbath, especially for Union soldiers. Johnston, however, was one of the Confederate casualties. General P.G.T. Beauregard quickly replaced him and continued the battle, lining up 62 cannons and firing on Union soldiers at point blank range.

As rain poured down throughout the cold night, the battlefield was littered with bodies of dead and dying soldiers. Afraid they would be shot if they came out of hiding, Union soldiers could do nothing to help their fallen comrades.

Union troops recapture artillery at the Battle of Shiloh in 1862.

The Union Army was suffering great defeat but did not give up. Grant hoped reinforcements would arrive. That evening, fresh Union soldiers did arrive with Wallace, who had taken the wrong road and was delayed. More reinforcements came with Union General Don Carlos Buell. The Confederates were now outnumbered. Grant wasted no time. He gathered his troops and pushed the Confederates back to the same place the battle had begun.

Meanwhile, Confederates troops retained control of the important Mississippi River by holding the city of Vicksburg,

> *The Battle of Shiloh (April 6-7, 1862) was the deadliest battle fought on American soil up to that time. The death toll was shocking—the North lost about 13,000 soldiers and the South 10,700. More Americans died in the Battle of Shiloh than in the Revolutionary War, the War of 1812, and the Mexican War combined. Bullets buzzed through the trees so rapidly during the fight that one field became known as the Hornet's Nest.*

Mississippi. Throughout the winter of 1862-1863, Grant's troops drew closer to this well protected Southern stronghold. If Vicksburg fell, the North would control the Mississippi River, which would divide the South in two.

Capturing Vicksburg would be no easy task. The river town sat high on a bluff with a brilliant view of the river valley and all that surrounded it. A surprise attack would be impossible. An assault from the north side of town was also impossible. Others had tried and failed. Grant decided he needed to get south of Vicksburg to make his move.

During the night on April 16, 1863, a fleet of Union gunboats and supply barges made their way along the Mississippi to Vicksburg. Grant knew a route where his troops could cross the river and make an assault on Vicksburg from the south. Although they suffered under heavy Confederate shelling, Union troops made it to their destination. The crossing put Grant's troops between two Confederate generals—General John C. Pemberton at Vicksburg and General Joe Johnston, who was bringing reinforcements.

Grant's troops kept the Confederates off guard, attacking one group and then the other. In less than three weeks of fighting, Union troops captured 6,000 soldiers and countless weapons. More important, Pemberton and his soldiers were trapped.

In May, Grant's men attacked the fort, but made no progress. A second attempt yielded the same result. Rather than lose more men needlessly, Grant decided to hold Vicksburg under siege. It had worked at Fort Donelson, and he believed it would work here, as well. It did. On July 3, 1863, Pemberton asked Grant for terms of surrender. Grant wanted the Confederates to surrender unconditionally, but Pemberton refused. Grant said the

30,000 men trapped at Vicksburg could go home to their families and resume their lives if they stacked their weapons and left them. Pemberton agreed, and the surrender became official July 4, 1863.

The Battle of Vicksburg ended when the Confederates surrendered on July 4, 1863.

When news of the Union victory reached the U.S. capital, Lincoln promoted Grant to major general. Soon Grant received orders to help Union troops under siege in Chattanooga, Tennessee.

Hearing that the great General Grant was on his way inspired Union troops. They had heard about Grant's victories and looked forward to his leadership. At Chattanooga, Confederates were in control of two key points—Lookout Mountain and Missionary Ridge. Once Union soldiers forced the rebels to abandon Lookout Mountain, Grant gave the troops permission to charge the rebels the next morning at Missionary Ridge. With vigor, Grant's men attacked the ridge and accomplished their mission. The siege ended, and supply lines for Chattanooga opened up.

In March 1864, Lincoln named Grant lieutenant general and gave him command of the entire Union Army. In this new position, Grant answered only to the president. That same month, Grant and Lincoln met face to face for the first time. The two made an odd-looking pair—the tall, slim president and the short general—but they got along right away. They both wanted the same thing—the end of the Civil War.

President Abraham Lincoln commissions Ulysses S. Grant as lieutenant general of the Union Army in 1864.

Without anyone to hinder him anymore, Grant got right to work. The Union still needed to defeat General Robert E. Lee's army in Virginia and General Joe Johnston's army in Tennessee. Grant would take on Lee.

In the spring of 1864, Grant moved his troops through Virginia, pushing General Lee back closer and closer to Richmond, the Confederate capital. The Union death toll mounted. After a particularly bloody five-day battle at Spotsylvania, Virginia, Grant wrote Julia about the horror of it all. "The world has never seen so bloody and so protracted a battle as the one being fought and I hope never will again."

Eventually, Grant's troops moved behind Lee's men and cut off their supplies. About 20 miles (32.2 km) south of Richmond in Petersburg, Union troops held strong and laid siege to the Confederates.

While Confederates were trapped at Petersburg, Grant brought in miners from the state of Pennsylvania to dig a long tunnel under the fort. After two weeks of digging, the miners finished their job. Union soldiers then placed 8,000 pounds of explosive powder at the end of the tunnel, right beneath the fort. On July 30, 1864, one soldier lit the fuse, but nothing happened.

Two brave men ventured back into the tunnel to find out what went wrong. The fuse had failed. The men relit the fuse and ran out of the tunnel as fast as

The front page of the New York Times, *April 4, 1865, tells of the Union's victory at Richmond.*

their legs could carry them. At 4:44 A.M., the powder exploded, sending a huge mushroom of fire and smoke into the air. Union soldiers were so frightened, they hesitated before charging the fort.

By the time Union soldiers started running through the huge crater made by the blast, they were easy targets for the remaining rebels. The Confederates just stood on the edge of the crater and shot them down.

The Confederates were able to defend their position there at Petersburg for about nine months. During those difficult months, both sides occasionally planned attacks, but nothing worked. It was only a matter of time, however, before the rebels became worn out and their supplies dwindled to nothing. By April 1865, Lee's men, deprived of additional food for nearly a year, stood on the brink of starvation. General Lee was ready to surrender.

Lee and Grant agreed to meet in the town of Appomattox Court House, Virginia, at the home of Wilmer McLean. Looking prim and proper in his crisp, clean uniform, Lee arrived at the house on April 9, 1865. Grant, dressed in a mud-spattered uniform, met Lee in the parlor. Immediately, the two military leaders began a friendly conversation about their many army experiences. Their

After the end of the Civil War, Confederate leader Robert E. Lee turned down several positions that would have made him a lot of money. Instead, he became the president of Washington College, now Washington and Lee University in Lexington, Virginia. He also worked to rebuild his home state of Virginia and reunite the country.

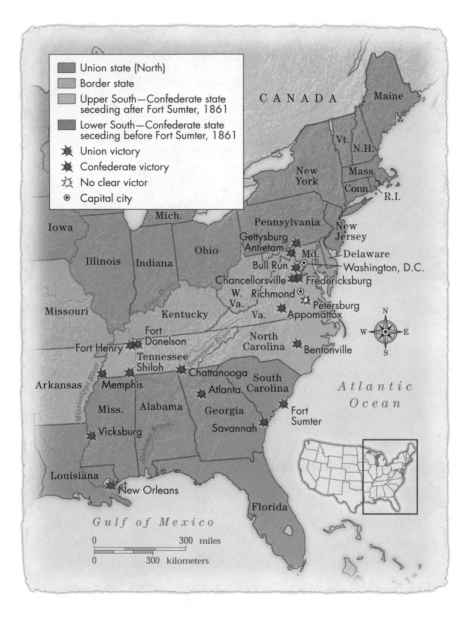

Union state (North)
Border state
Upper South—Confederate state seceding after Fort Sumter, 1861
Lower South—Confederate state seceding before Fort Sumter, 1861
✺ Union victory
✺ Confederate victory
✺ No clear victor
⊛ Capital city

CANADA   Maine

Vt.
N.H.

New York   Mass.
Conn.
R.I.

Iowa   Mich.   Pennsylvania   New Jersey

Gettysburg
Antietam   Md.   Delaware

Ohio   Bull Run   Washington, D.C.

Illinois   Indiana   Chancellorsville   Fredericksburg

W.   Richmond ⊛
Va.   Va.   Petersburg
Appomattox

Missouri   Kentucky

Fort Donelson   North Carolina   Bentonville
Fort Henry   Tennessee
Shiloh   Chattanooga   South Carolina
Arkansas   Memphis   Atlanta
Miss.   Alabama   Georgia   Fort Sumter
Vicksburg   Savannah

Louisiana   Atlantic Ocean

New Orleans   Florida

Gulf of Mexico

0   300 miles
0   300 kilometers

Civil War battles were fought in Union and Confederate states (map shows modern boundaries).

conversation was so pleasant, they almost forgot why they were there.

Soon, the talk turned to surrender, and Grant

wrote down his terms. Lee accepted the conditions, and the documents of surrender were signed.

Sympathetic to Lee's defeat, Grant stopped his men from firing their guns in a show of victory and agreed to send food to the starving men of the Confederate Army. He knew it was time for the country to begin to heal.

Five days after Lee's surrender, Grant was in Washington, D.C., meeting with President Lincoln's

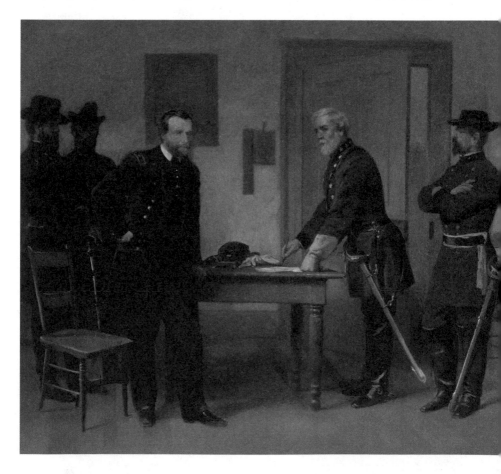

Confederate General Robert E. Lee (right of table) surrendered to Union General Ulysses S. Grant at Appomattox Courthouse, Virginia, on April 9, 1865.

cabinet to discuss the future of the South. That night, on April 14, 1865, John Wilkes Booth assassinated President Lincoln at Ford's Theatre in Washington, D.C. Already on his way to New Jersey to meet his family, Grant heard the news as he got off a ferry on the Delaware River. Deeply saddened by the news, he immediately arranged to return to Washington, D.C., where he found the people of the city in deep shock and grief.

> The day Lincoln was assassinated during a play at Ford's Theatre in Washington, D.C., President and Mrs. Lincoln had invited Ulysses S. Grant and his wife Julia to accompany them. Longing to get home to his children in New Jersey, Grant declined the president's invitation. As a result, John Wilkes Booth's plan to assassinate Grant along with Lincoln was prevented.

Grant feared what Lincoln's death would do to a nation that was already divided and broken. He grieved that the country would not benefit from Lincoln's efforts to grant equal rights and full citizenship to all people. He also feared that Vice President Andrew Johnson, who would succeed Lincoln as president, would not work hard enough for the Southern people. Grant was not convinced that Johnson would achieve post-war unity and reconstruction.

Grant was very popular after the war. About six months after Lincoln's death, Grant toured the nation, receiving praise everywhere he went. President Johnson even asked Grant to tour the

South. To Grant's surprise, Southerners greeted him with friendliness.

On July 25, 1866, Congress established a new military rank—general of the armies of the United States. It was no surprise that Grant was appointed to this new prominent position. All military orders given by the president had to be approved by the general of the armies—Ulysses S. Grant. ❧

Assassin John Wilkes Booth sneaked into Lincoln's box at Ford's Theatre on April 14, 1865.

8 PRESIDENT GRANT

ↄᴄ✕ᴐↄ

It wasn't long before Ulysses S. Grant's popularity and position took him straight to the White House. The boy who didn't know what job would suit him was now one of the most admired men in America.

Ulysses S. Grant was elected president of the United States in 1868, followed by a second term in 1872. Unfortunately, he was a better soldier than a president. His presidency got off to a bad start when he chose his cabinet without discussing it with other Republican leaders. He often surrounded himself with people who were easily corrupted, and his terms in office were scarred by financial scandals.

"Our eight years in the Executive Mansion were delightful, but there were some dark clouds in the bright sky," Julia wrote later in her memoirs. "There

Financial chaos broke out on the New York Stock Exchange on Black Friday, September 24, 1869.

was that dreadful Black Friday."

Black Friday started with a scheme to control the U.S. gold market. James Fisk and Jay Gould were businessmen and investors who were often involved in scandals and corrupt business deals. In 1869, they devised a plan to buy all the gold they could get their hands on. That would force bankers and other businessmen to buy gold from them at whatever high price they chose. However, the plan wouldn't work if the federal government decided to compete with them and sell its gold at a lower price. Fisk and Gould created a financial panic in the entire country on September 24, 1869—Black Friday—when the high price of gold caused a nationwide scare. However, Grant quickly ordered the federal government to sell its gold, which brought the price of gold back down.

Another dark cloud of Grant's presidency involved the conflict between the Indians and the white settlers moving west. Attempting to protect their land, Indians sometimes attacked the settlers, and U.S. troops sent to protect the settlers could be brutal to the Indians. Thinking it would help them, Grant called for placing the Indians on reservations so they could learn about white culture and farming methods. Reservation land was often dry and infertile, however, and many Indians became reliant on the government.

> *A variety of treaties eventually gave some rights to Native Americans. The Indian Citizenship Act of 1924 granted citizenship to all who were born within the United States. As citizens, American Indians now had the right to vote.*

One of Grant's biggest challenges was to protect the rights of former slaves. He supported the 15th Amendment to the U.S. Constitution, approved on February 3, 1870, which gave black men the right to vote. Some Southern states still found ways to deny them that right, however. Hatred toward black people grew in the South, providing a setting for groups like the Ku Klux Klan to form. The Ku Klux Klan worked to deny rights to former slaves and often terrorized blacks throughout the country. Empowered by the Force Acts of 1870-1871, which ensured the right of all citizens to vote, Grant sent troops to the South to protect voters. He also ordered the Ku Klux Klan in South Carolina to disband and surrender to federal troops. It would be almost a century, though, before blacks in the South had the same rights as whites.

Despite the conflicts and scandals of his presi-

Political cartoon showing a member of the White League and a member of the Ku Klux Klan joining hands over a terrorized black family.

IN FOR IT.
U. S. "I hope I shall get to the bottom soon."

This cartoon mocks Grant's second term in office for its seemingly endless string of scandals.

dency, Grant did make some great strides. Under his leadership, an important deal was made with Britain. An international panel of judges decided Britain should pay the United States $15.5 million for helping the Confederates make warships during the Civil War. This was one of the greatest accomplishments of Grant's presidency. He also established the country's first national park—Yellowstone National Park—on March 1, 1872. While much remained to be done after Grant left office, his country still respected him. ❧

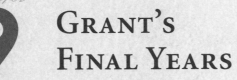

9 GRANT'S FINAL YEARS

—∾—

After serving eight difficult years as president, Ulysses S. Grant and his wife Julia needed a well-deserved vacation. He made plans to whisk Julia and their 19-year-old son Jesse off to Europe.

Bound for Great Britain, the Grants set sail from Philadelphia, Pennsylvania, aboard the *Indiana* on May 17, 1877. Grant's reception in England surprised him. Crowds struggled to get a glimpse of the Civil War hero and cheered his visit. In Newcastle, England, about 80,000 people participated in a huge parade in his honor. Hard-working English people knew about Grant's simple upbringing and appreciated his modest charm. In return, Grant enjoyed meeting factory workers, farmers, and other everyday people much more than meeting royalty.

Ulysses S. Grant works on his Memoirs *during his final days in 1885.*

Grant basked in the adoration the people of England showered upon him. He spoke to them about things they wanted to hear—his adventures as a soldier more than his time as president. Grant assured them that war was not glamorous, nor something he enjoyed. He wrote:

> *I was always a man of peace, and I have advocated peace, although educated a soldier. I never willingly, although I have gone through two war[s], on my own accord advocated war.*

The Grants ended up having such a good time, the trip turned into a two-year, around-the-world adventure. In the next two years, they traveled to many countries, including Switzerland, Italy, France, Egypt, India, Russia, China, and Japan. They enjoyed their adventures, but the time finally came in September 1879 for them to return and resume life in the United States.

After serving two terms as president of the United States, Grant became president of the Mexican Southern Railroad Company. He encouraged trade between Mexico and the United States and entered into a trade agreement with Mexico in 1882 and 1883.

When he got home, Grant found some of his friends planning his return to the presidency. Feeling he had already done his duty for his county, Grant was

Grant returned from his trip to England in 1879 to a huge reception at the Palace Hotel in San Francisco, California.

ready to settle into life as a private citizen. On the other hand, he did not want to disappoint his friends. Since presidential terms were not limited then to two terms, Grant agreed to run for a third term in the 1880 election. However, after delegates at the Republican National Convention cast 36 ballots, they voted narrowly to nominate James Garfield as their presidential candidate. Instead of being disappointed, Grant was relieved.

With his days of public service behind him, Grant

still needed to earn money. His family's long vacation had nearly dried up his savings. Grant thought he might earn some money by investing the money he still had, so he gave the money to an investment company formed by his son Ulysses Jr. and a man named Ferdinand Ward. Grant even borrowed money from a man named W. H. Vanderbilt to help out his son's new business called Grant and Ward.

Ward, however, was not an honest man and would take a client's money and pretend to invest it. Meanwhile, he'd get others to invest, too, and use their money to pay the first investor. Eventually, the scheme caught up with Ward, but in the meantime, the former president lost all of his savings.

After Ward disappeared with the money, Grant still had to pay back Vanderbilt's loan. He insisted that Vanderbilt accept his New York home, his farm near St. Louis, and his mementoes from the Civil War as payment. Vanderbilt felt sorry for Grant but didn't turn down the offer.

Not long after the Grant and Ward scandal, Ulysses S. Grant became ill. He noticed his throat hurt when he ate. Eventually, the pain didn't go away, and he soon discovered he had cancer. When Grant got the news he was going to die, he immediately thought of his family. The loss of his savings and property in the Grant and Ward scam had left the family virtually penniless. He worried about

Ulysses S. Grant during his final days at Mount McGregor, New York

how they would have enough money to survive after he was gone.

Grant came up with a plan. Before he died, he would write the story of his life. He was a popular man, and people would like to read about his adventures in the Mexican War and the Civil War, as well as his time as president. He believed the money made from the book would keep his family comfortable.

Before he started writing, Grant contacted one of his friends, Mark Twain. A famous author and publisher, Twain was more than happy to help out his friend. He agreed to publish Grant's memoirs and gave the dying man $25,000 before it was even written. Once the book was published, the Grants would earn 70 percent of the profits, which eventually made the family $500,000.

Knowing he had little time left, Grant got right to work. On February 25, 1885, he propped himself up with pillows and started writing. When the weather permitted, Grant sat on a chair on the porch of his home, working on his life story. Since he was still a popular figure among Americans of his day, many people stopped at his home to hear updates on his health. Well-wishers waited outside to see the former president smile and wave from his window on days he felt strong enough to leave his bed. People paused to pay their respects but didn't interrupt the former president as he wrote. His time was short, and he refused to die before his book was done.

The completed *Personal Memoirs of U.S. Grant* went to the publisher in May. Grant had met his goal, although writing toward the end of his life was difficult. In June, to avoid the summer heat, the Grants moved to a cottage in Mount McGregor, New York, in the Adirondack Mountains. About

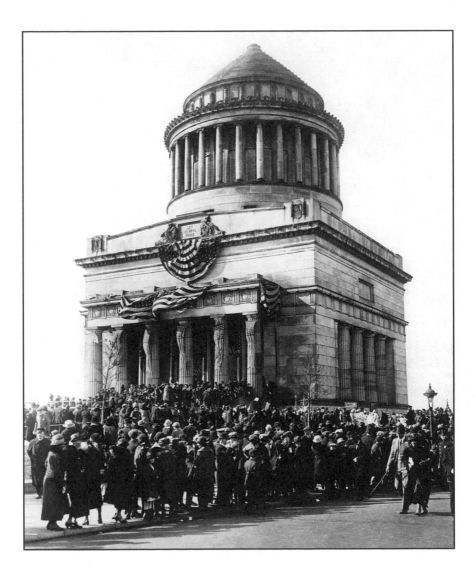

one month later, on July 23, 1885, Ulysses S. Grant quietly died in his Mount McGregor home, at the age of 63, surrounded by all his loving family. Knowing he had provided for his family's future, the war hero and president could now rest. ☙

In April 1922, crowds gathered at Grant's tomb in New York City to commemorate the 100th anniversary of his birth.

GRANT'S LIFE

1843

graduates from the U.S. Military Academy at West Point, New York

1845

leaves Louisiana to go to Texas with the 4th U.S. Infantry to fight in the Mexican War

1822

born in Point Pleasant, Ohio

1820

1840

Auguste Rodin, famous sculptor of *The Thinker*, is born

1823

Mexico becomes a republic

1846

Irish potato famine reaches its worst

German astronomer Johann Gottfried Galle discovers Neptune

WORLD EVENTS

1850

first child, Frederick
Dent Grant, is born

1852

is transferred to the
Pacific Coast; his
second son, Ulysses
S. Grant Jr., is born
while he is away
from his family

1848

marries Julia Dent
August 22 in St. Louis,
Missouri

1850

1848

*The Communist
Manifesto*, by German
writer Karl Marx, is
widely distributed

1850

Jeans are invented
by Levi Strauss, a
German who moved
to America during
the gold rush

1852

American Harriet
Beecher Stowe
publishes *Uncle
Tom's Cabin*

Life and Times

GRANT'S LIFE

1854
resigns from
the Army

1855
daughter, Ellen
Wrenshall Grant,
is born

1858
son, Jesse Root
Grant Jr., is born

1856
Nikola Tesla, electri-
cal engineer and
inventor, is born

The Treaty of Paris
ends the Crimean
War

1858
English scientist Charles
Darwin presents his
theory of evolution

1857
E.G. Otis installs the
first safety elevator
in the United States

WORLD EVENTS

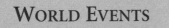

1862

leads attacks on Fort Henry and Fort Donelson in Tennessee early in the year, followed by the Battle of Shiloh in April

1863

siege of Vicksburg ends with Confederate surrender July 4

1861

joins the Union Army at the start of the Civil War and is appointed brigadier general

1860

1860

Austrian composer Gustav Mahler is born in Kalischt (now in Austria)

GRANT'S LIFE

1864

promoted to lieutenant general and given command of entire Union Army; begins march toward General Robert E. Lee's forces in Richmond, Virginia

1865

accepts Confederate surrender April 9 at Appomattox Court House, Virginia, initiating the end of the Civil War

1868

elected to first term as president of the United States of America

1865

Lewis Carroll writes *Alice's Adventures in Wonderland*

1868

Louisa May Alcott publishes *Little Women*

WORLD EVENTS

1872
reelected as president of the United States of America

1877
leaves with wife Julia and son Jesse for two-year trip around the world

1885
dies of throat cancer July 23 in Mount McGregor, New York

1870

1880

1869
The periodic table of elements is invented

The transcontinental railroad across the United States is completed

1876
The Battle of the Little Bighorn is a victory for Native Americans defending their homes in the West against General George Custer

Alexander Graham Bell uses the first telephone to speak to his assistant, Thomas Watson

1884
Mark Twain publishes *The Adventures of Hucklelberry Finn*

DATE OF BIRTH: April 27, 1822

BIRTHPLACE: Point Pleasant, Ohio

FATHER: Jesse Root Grant
(1794-1873)

MOTHER: Hannah Simpson Grant
(1798-1883)

EDUCATION: Georgetown, Ohio, until 14;
Richeson and Rand
Academy, Maysville,
Kentucky, one year;
School in Ripley, Ohio, one
year;
U.S. Military Academy, West
Point, New York, four years,
graduated 1843

SPOUSE: Julia Dent Grant
(1826-1902)

DATE OF
MARRIAGE: August 22, 1848

CHILDREN: Frederick Dent Grant
(1850-1912);
Ulysses S. Grant Jr.
(1852-1928);
Ellen Wrenshall Grant
(1855-1922);
Jesse Root Grant Jr.
(1858-1934)

DATE OF DEATH: July 23, 1885

PLACE OF BURIAL: General Grant National
Memorial in New York City

In the Library

Archer, Jules. *A House Divided: The Lives of Ulysses S. Grant and Robert E. Lee.* New York: Scholastic Paperbacks, 1997.

Davis, Todd. *New Big Book of U.S. Presidents.* Philadelphia: Courage Books, 2000.

Fitz-Gerald, Christine. *Julia Dent Grant.* Danbury, Conn.: Children's Press, 1998.

King, David C. *Ulysses S. Grant.* Woodbridge, Conn.: Blackbirch Press, 2001.

Nardo, Don. *The Mexican-American War.* San Diego: Lucent Books, 1999.

O'Shei, Tim, and Arthur Meier Schlesinger. *Ulysses S. Grant: Military Leader and President.* Broomhall, Pa.: Chelsea House, 2001.

Williams, Jean Kinney. *Ulysses S. Grant.* Minneapolis: Compass Point Books, 2003.

On the Web

For more information on *Ulysses S. Grant*, use FactHound to track down Web sites related to this book.

1. Go to *www.facthound.com*
2. Type in a search word related to this book or this book ID: 0756508207
3. Click on the *Fetch It* button.

FactHound will find the best Web sites for you.

Historic Sites

Ulysses S. Grant National Historic Site
7400 Grant Road
St. Louis, MO 63123
314/842-1867
A two-story frame house named "White Haven" where Grant lived. The house honors his life, military career, and political career.

General Grant National Memorial
122nd Street and Riverside Drive
New York, NY 10027
212/666-1640
The tomb of Ulysses S. Grant and his wife Julia Dent Grant

Glossary

abolitionists
people who worked to get rid of slavery

annex
to take over a territory and add it to a country or state

apprenticed
working for and learning from a skilled worker for a certain amount of time

cavalry
soldiers who ride horses

celerity
quick action

cholera
a disease of the digestive system, caused by bacteria

Confederacy
the Southern states that fought against the Northern states in the Civil War; also called the Confederate States of America

memoirs
written memories from a person's life

nominated
chosen to run for election

patriots
people who love their country and support it

quartermaster
military officer in charge of getting supplies to the troops

rebels
soldiers of the Confederate Army during the Civil War who fought against the U.S. government

regiment
a military group made up of several battalions

secede
to formally withdraw from an organization, state, or country

siege
an operation where an army surrounds a place to force surrender

tannery
a place where animal skins are tanned, or changed into leather

telegram
a message sent by code over connecting wires

tuberculosis
a serious bacterial disease that affects the lungs

unconditional
complete and absolute with no terms or conditions

Union
the Northern states that fought against the Southern states in the Civil War

Chapter 2

Page 17, line 25: William S. McFeely. *Grant*. Norwalk, Conn.: Easton Press, 1987, pp. 10-11.

Page 18, line 17: Ibid., p. 11.

Chapter 3

Page 25, line 11: Ibid., p. 16.

Page 26, line 2: Henry Thomas. *Ulysses S. Grant*. New York: Putnam, 1961, p. 25.

Chapter 4

Page 30, line 13: *Grant* (McFeely), p. 23.

Page 33, line 22: Ibid., p. 38.

Page 35, line 1: Ibid., p. 29.

Page 35, line 21: Ibid., p. 39.

Chapter 5

Page 45, line 12: *Grant* (McFeely), p. 52.

Page 45, line 23: Ibid., p. 54.

Page 48, line 1: Ibid., p. 61.

Chapter 6

Page 53, line 14: Ibid., p. 70.

Page 55, line 26 Ibid., p. 72.

Page 57, line 18: Ibid., p. 80.

Page 58, line 6: Ibid., p. 84.

Page 59, line 1: Ibid., p. 81.

Page 61, line 2: Ibid., p. 97.

Page 61, line 27: Ibid., p. 104.

Page 63, line 13: Ibid., p. 106.

Page 64, line 7: Ibid., p. 109.

Page 65, line 9: Ibid., p. 109.

Page 66, line 4: Ibid., p. 110.

Chapter 7

Page 75, line 11: Ibid., p. 169.

Chapter 8

Page 83, line 13: Jean Edward Smith. *Grant*. New York: Simon & Schuster, 2001, p. 406.

Chapter 9

Page 90, line 7: *Grant* (McFeely), p. 2.

Select Bibliography

"General Grant." *National Park Service.* http://www.nps.gov/gegr/index.htm.

"Grant, Ulysses S(impson)." *Encarta.* http://encarta.msn.com/encyclopedia_761555289/Grant_Ulysses_S(impson).html

"Grant, Ulysses Simpson." *The New Book of Knowledge.* http://ap.grolier.com/article?assetid=a2012170-h&templatename=/article/article.html.

"In His Shoes: Child of the Frontier." *American Experience.* http://www.pbs.org/wgbh/amex/grant/broadband/ihs_text_01.html.

"Julia Dent Grant." *The White House.* http://www.whitehouse.gov/history/firstladies/jg18.html.

McFeely, William S. *Grant.* Norwalk, Conn.: Easton Press, 1987.

"People & Events: Ulysses S. Grant." *American Experience.* http://www.pbs.org/wgbh/amex/grant/peopleevents/p_ugrant.html.

"Presidential Places: Ulysses S. Grant." *American Presidents.* http://www.americanpresidents.org/places/18c.asp.

Smith, Jean Edward. *Grant.* New York: Simon & Schuster, 2001.

Thomas, Henry. *Ulysses S. Grant.* New York: Putnam, 1961.

"Ulysses S. Grant." *The White House.* http://www.whitehouse.gov/history/presidents/ug18.html.

"Ulysses S. Grant." *The World Almanac for Kids.* http://www.worldalmanacforkids.com/explore/presidents/grant_ulysses.html

Brenda Haugen is the author and editor of many books, most of them for children. A graduate of the University of North Dakota in Grand Forks, Brenda lives in North Dakota with her family.

Image Credits